TARLA DALAL

India's #1 Cookery Author

Sizzlers & Barbeques

S&C

SANJAY & CO
MUMBAI

- Other Books by Tarla Dalal -

INDIAN COOKING
Tava Cooking
Rotis & Subzis
Desi Khana
The Complete Gujarati Cook Book
Mithai
Chaat
Achaar aur Parathe
The Rajasthani Cookbook
Swadisht Subzian

WESTERN COOKING
The Complete Italian Cookbook
The Chocolate Cookbook
Eggless Desserts
Mocktails & Snacks
Soups & Salads
Mexican Cooking
Easy Gourmet Cooking
Chinese Cooking
Easy Chinese Cooking
Thai Cooking

MINI SERIES
Idlis & Dosas
Cooking under 10 minutes
Pizzas and Pasta
Fun Food for Children
Roz Ka Khana
Microwave - Desi Khana
T.V. Meals
Paneer
Parathas
Chawal
Dals

Sandwiches
Quick Cooking
Curries & Kadhis
Chinese Recipes
Jain Desi Khana
7 Dinner Menus
Jain International Recipes
Punjabi Subzis
Corn
Microwave Subzis
Baked Dishes New
Stir-Fry New

TOTAL HEALTH
Low Calorie Healthy Cooking
Pregnancy Cookbook
Baby and Toddler Cookbook
Cooking with 1 Teaspoon of Oil
Home Remedies
Delicious Diabetic Recipes
Fast Foods Made Healthy
Healthy Soups & Salads
Healthy Breakfast
Calcium Rich Recipes
Healthy Heart Cook Book
Forever Young Diet

Healthy Snacks
Iron Rich Recipes
Healthy Juices
Low Cholesterol Recipes
Good Food for Diabetes
Healthy Subzis
Healthy Snacks for Kids
High Blood Pressure Cook Book
Low Calorie Sweets
Nutritious Recipes for Pregnancy
Diabetic Snacks New
Zero Oil Rotis & Subzis New
Zero Oil Soups, Salads & Snacks New

GENERAL COOKING
Exciting Vegetarian Cooking
Microwave Recipes
Quick & Easy Cooking
Saatvik Khana
Mixer Cook Book
The Pleasures of Vegetarian Cooking
The Delights of Vegetarian Cooking
The Joys of Vegetarian Cooking
Cooking with Kids
Snacks Under 10 Minutes
Ice-Cream & Frozen Desserts
Desserts Under 10 Minutes
Entertaining
Microwave Snacks & Desserts

Third Printing : 2007

ISBN 10 : 81-86469-72-9
ISBN 13 : 978-8-186469-72-9

Price Rs. 149/-

Published & distributed by
SANJAY & COMPANY
A-1, 353 Shah & Nahar Industrial Estate, Dhanraj Mill Compound, Lower Parel (W), Mumbai 400 013, INDIA.
Tel: (91-22) 2496 8068 / Fax: (91-22) 2496 5876 / Email: sanjay@tarladalal.com / Website: www.tarladalal.com

UK and USA customers can call us on :
UK : 02080029533 • USA : 213-634-1406
For books, Membership on **tarladalal.com**, Subscription for **Cooking & More** and Recipe queries
Timing : 9.30 a.m. to 7.00 p.m. (IST), from Monday to Saturday
Local call charges applicable

Recipe Research & Production Design Pinky Dixit Arati Kamat Fedane Pradnya Sundararaj	**Food Stylist** Saba Gaziyani	**Photography** Sandeep Mhatre	**Design** Satyamangal Rege	**Printed by** Minal Sales Agencies, Mumbai

INTRODUCTION

Dear Friends,

This time I bring to you two rather unusual subjects.......SIZZLERS and BARBEQUES, which are particularly close to my heart.

Sizzlers are a recent *'inno-vention'* that consist of an entire meal being served on a cast iron platter, which is in turn placed on a wooden base.

Sizzlers probably originated a few centuries ago when meat was served on a heated cast iron plate to keep it piping hot, while the diner ate his meal. Today, however, they have become a cuisine of sorts by themselves as many specialty restaurants serve only Sizzlers on their menu. A sizzler is a combination of a main dish served with a choice of sauces and a large variety of accompaniments, making it a complete meal by itself!

The sizzlers featured here are inspired by a variety of world cuisines—great authentic recipes presented in a creative manner, resulting in innovative recipes. We have let loose the reins of our imagination to come up with mouthwatering, delectable combinations. Once you've gorged yourselves with these, I am sure you can create your own hot favourites

I love the tantalizing aroma of a well-made sizzler. Italian, Thai, Indonesian and Indian are among a few of the sizzlers I have enjoyed most.... both cooking, as well as eating! so they have found a place in this book.. Also included are some yummy dessert sizzlers among them my favorite, the fudgy brownies served with marinated fruits and warm chocolate sauce.

Barbeques are for outdoor cooking using the ancient technique of open fire and smoke and 'where there is smoke, there is bound to be flavour!' The barbeque season kick starts during the winter here in India and in the summer abroad. This is the time to dig out the charcoal, scrub down the barbecue and enjoy the great outdoors surrounded by friends and lots of enticing food sizzling over the fire. However, often vegetarians who are invited to barbeques end up with a very limited selection of foods, as most barbecued dishes are meat based. Even at cocktail parties, the vegetarian fare is restricted to unexciting bites like peanuts, cashew nuts and pakodas.

Time to forget this discomfort. You will find a slew of vegetarian barbecue recipes in the section on 'Barbeques and Grills', which has a delectable selection of vegetarian appetizers that include more than the usual tandoori marinade. These easy-to- make dishes can be prepared in a jiffy, for those unexpected guests ...and will speak volumes about your culinary skills.

Another advantage is that you do not necessarily have to only grill or barbeque these dishes...you can also sauté them in a pan, making your work a lot easier...you will only miss the smoky flavour that barbeque grills impart!

All these scrumptious, finger licking recipes are simple to prepare and easy to eat.... and eat!

Happy cooking and grilling ...

Cheers,

Tarla Dalal

Sizzlers

Barbeques & Grills

Sauces & Dips

Sizzlers

Sizzlers are meant for small gatherings, as they are sit down meals. Prepare the sizzler platters by heating the cast iron dishes in an oven or over an open flame till they are hot. Lift the dishes carefully (remember to put on your oven mitts or better watch out........!) and place them onto the wooden base. Pile up the food on to the plate, drizzle the oil and water mixture on top and presto .....hear the hzzzzz...... of a dramatic 'sizzle'.....the one that this dish is known after! Sizzler platters are easily available at most wholesale markets, at all the metros in India.

PANEER TIKKA SIZZLER

Picture on page 9

Preparation time :
15 minutes.

Cooking time :
60 minutes.

Makes 2 sizzlers.

Succulent pieces of paneer marinated in a tantalizing tandoori masala grilled to perfection and served with pulao, a stuffed capsicum and tangy makhani gravy. If you like, serve some grilled onions with it too.

For the paneer tikkas
1½ cups paneer (cottage cheese), cut into 50 mm. (2") cubes
½ cup onions, cut into thick wedges
½ cup capsicum, cut into 50 mm. (2") pieces
½ cup thick curds
½ teaspoon Bengal gram flour (besan)
1 teaspoon ginger paste
1 teaspoon garlic paste
2 teaspoons chilli powder
½ teaspoon kasuri methi (dried fenugreek leaves)
½ teaspoon garam masala
2 tablespoons chopped coriander
2 tablespoons mustard oil
salt to taste

For the yellow rice
1 cup long grained rice
½ teaspoon cumin seeds (jeera)
25 mm. (1") stick cinnamon (dalchini)
2 cloves (laung)
1 bay leaf (tej patta)
¼ teaspoon turmeric powder (haldi)
1 tablespoon oil
salt to taste

For the makhani sauce
5 large tomatoes, roughly chopped
2 cloves (laung)
4 to 5 cashewnuts
½ teaspoon cumin seeds (jeera)
2 teaspoons ginger-garlic paste
½ cup onions, finely chopped
1 teaspoon chilli powder
3 tablespoons cream
¼ teaspoon garam masala
½ teaspoon kasuri methi (dried fenugreek leaves)

7

1 tablespoon oil
1 tablespoon butter
salt to taste

For the stuffed capsicum
1 capsicum
½ cup corn kernels, boiled
½ cup green peas, boiled
½ teaspoon roasted cumin seed (jeera) powder
1 teaspoon chopped coriander
salt to taste

Other ingredients
1 tablespoon oil mixed with 1 tablespoon of water

For the paneer tikkas

1. Combine the curds, gram flour, ginger paste, garlic paste, chilli powder, kasuri methi, garam masala, coriander, salt and 1 tablespoon of mustard oil and mix well to prepare a marinade.
2. Add the paneer, onions and capsicum to it and keep aside for 10 to 15 minutes.
3. Arrange the paneer, onions and capsicum on 4 skewer sticks.
4. Heat the balance 1 tablespoon of mustard oil on a non-stick tava (griddle) and sauté the paneer tikkas on all sides till they are lightly browned (approximately 4 to 5 minutes).

PANEER TIKKA SIZZLER, *page 7.*

For the yellow rice
1. Clean, wash and soak the rice for 10 minutes. Drain and keep aside.
2. Heat the oil in a heavy bottomed pan, add the cumin seeds, cloves and bay leaf and stir.
3. When the seeds crackle, add the rice, turmeric powder and salt and sauté for 2 minutes.
4. Add 2 cups of hot water. Cover and cook over a slow flame for 10 to 15 minutes till the rice is cooked. Keep aside.

For the makhani sauce
1. Combine the tomatoes, cloves, cashewnuts and oil with ¼ cup water and simmer for 15 to 20 minutes. Cool completely.
2. Blend to a smooth purée in a liquidiser. Strain the purée through a sieve and keep aside.
3. Melt the butter in a pan and add the cumin seeds.
4. When the seeds crackle, add the ginger-garlic paste and sauté for a few seconds.
5. Add the onions and sauté till the onions turn golden brown.
6. Add the strained purée, chilli powder, cream, garam masala, kasuri methi and salt and bring it to a boil. Keep aside.

For the stuffed capsicum
1. Cut the capsicum into 2 halves horizontally, scoop out the seeds to create an empty shell.
2. Parboil the capsicum in salted water, drain and keep aside.
3. Combine the corn, peas, cumin seed powder, coriander and salt and mix well.
4. Fill this mixture in the capsicum halves and keep aside till required.

How to proceed
1. Heat 2 sizzler plates over an open flame till they are red hot and place them on their respective wooden trays.
2. Arrange half the warm yellow rice in the centre of each cast iron plate.
3. Place one stuffed capsicum on one side of each sizzler plate.
4. Top with 2 skewers of the paneer tikkas.
5. Repeat with the remaining ingredients on the other sizzler plate to make another sizzler.
6. Pour the oil-water mixture over the cast iron plates for a sizzling effect. Serve immediately with the makhani sauce.

INDONESIAN SIZZLER

This sizzler is laden with a bounty of flavours and spices. A delicately flavoured rice noodle preparation is topped with a smoky, curry flavoured satay, grilled and served with a spicy-sweet peanut sauce and crispy potatoes.

Preparation time :
30 minutes.

Cooking time :
30 minutes.

Makes 2 sizzlers.

For the peanut sauce
¼ cup onions, finely chopped
2 large cloves garlic, chopped
1 cup coconut milk
4 tablespoons peanut butter
rind of ½ lemon
1 stalk lemon grass
1 teaspoon chilli powder
1½ teaspoons brown sugar
juice of 1 lemon
1 teaspoon oil
salt to taste

For the satay
1 cup paneer, cubed
½ cup capsicum, diced
1 cup mushrooms, halved
½ cup peanut sauce, recipe above
2 teaspoons curry powder
salt to taste

For the noodles
2 cups cooked rice noodles
1 cup onions, sliced
1 teaspoon ginger paste
1 to 2 green chillies, finely chopped
½ cup carrots and french beans, chopped and boiled
1 tablespoon soya sauce
¼ cup chopped coriander
1 teaspoon oil
salt to taste

For the crispy potatoes
2 cups potato, peeled and cut into strips
2 teaspoons ginger-garlic paste

1 green chilli, sliced
1 tablespoon soya sauce
1 teaspoon cornflour
¼ teaspoon sugar
¼ cup chopped coriander
½ cup spring onions, chopped
1 teaspoon oil
salt to taste
oil for deep frying

Other ingredients
3 to 4 sago wafers, fried
1 tablespoon oil mixed with 1 tablespoon of water

For the peanut sauce
1. Heat the oil and sauté the onions and garlic till they are translucent.
2. Add the coconut milk, peanut butter and ½ cup water and bring to a boil.
3. Simmer and add the lemon rind, lemon grass, chilli powder, brown sugar, lemon juice and salt and simmer for 4 to 5 minutes. keep aside. Remove and discard the lemon grass.

For the satay
1. Combine all the ingredients in a bowl and allow them to marinate for 10 to 15 minutes.
2. Thread them onto 4 skewer sticks and grill them for 5 to 7 minutes over a high flame till they are lightly browned. Keep aside.

For the noodles
1. Heat the oil and sauté the onions, ginger paste and green chillies.
2. When the onions turn pink, add the carrots and french beans and sauté for a few minutes.
3. Add the noodles, soya sauce and salt and mix well over a high flame.
4. Top with the chopped coriander and keep aside.

For the crispy potatoes
1. Deep fry the potatoes in hot oil till they are crisp. Drain on absorbent paper and keep aside.
2. In a small bowl, combine the soya sauce, cornflour, sugar and salt with 1 tablespoon of water and keep aside.
3. Heat 1 teaspoon of oil in a pan and sauté the ginger-garlic paste and green chilli. Add the potatoes and soya sauce mixture and mix well over a high flame. Adjust the seasoning if required.
4. Top with the coriander and spring onions and keep aside.

TARLA DALAL
INDIA'S #1 COOKERY AUTHOR

Cooking & more

Make your pick for an annual subscription and avail off special discounts

Cost of Subscription	Free Gift	Total	Discount	You Save	You Pay
Rs. 50 per issue * 6 = Rs. 300	2 months membership of tarladalal.com worth Rs.200	Rs. 500	50%	Rs. 250	Rs. 250
Rs. 50 per issue * 6 = Rs. 300	NIL	Rs. 300	30%	Rs. 90	RS. 210

Tick below on any one of the boxes :

☐ Rs. 250 + Rs. 90 (shipping charges) = Rs. 340

☐ Rs. 210 + Rs. 90 (shipping charges) = Rs. 300

Conditions Apply. Offer valid for shipments in India only.
For overseas shipment please log on to www.tarladalal.com

SUBSCRIBE NOW & SAVE UPTO 50%

Please fill in your details below and send us along with a cheque of Rs. 300/- or Rs. 340/- (depending on your discount scheme chosen) payable in the name of "Sanjay & Co." addressed to Sanjay & Co., 353, A-1, Shah & Nahar Ind. Estate, Dhanraj Mills Compound, Lower Parel - West, Mumbai - 400013. INDIA.

Name : ....

Address : ....

....

City : .... Pin Code : ....

E-mail address : .... Tel.No. : ....

Please ensure to fill all the details to avoid any delay in the shipments of the magazine.
For any queries mail us at subscription@tarladalal.com or call us at 022-2496 8068. Conditions Apply.

How to proceed

1. Heat 2 sizzler plates over an open flame till they are red hot and place them on their respective wooden trays.
2. Arrange half the noodles on one plate and top with two warm satay skewers.
3. Place half the potatoes on the rest of the plate.
4. Reheat the peanut sauce, adding some water to adjust the consistency and pour over the satay skewers and noodles.
5. Repeat with the remaining ingredients on the other sizzler plate to make another sizzler.
6. Pour the oil-water mixture over the cast iron plates for a sizzling effect.
7. Top with the fried sago wafers and serve immdiately.

Picture on facing page

Preparation time :
15 minutes.

Cooking time :
60 minutes.

Makes 2 sizzlers.

Thai cooking is a tempting blend of Indian, Chinese and Malay cooking. Varying form the soothing coconut to fiery chillies, these flavours of Thailand on one platter are sure to stimulate your tastebuds and your appetite too!

For the sweet corn cutlets
1½ cups tender sweet corn kernels, raw
1 to 2 tablespoons red curry paste, recipe on page 16
2 teaspoons soya sauce
1 to 2 tablespoons rice flour
salt to taste
oil for deep frying

For the green rice
1 cup long grained rice
1 bay leaf
4 tablespoons chopped coriander
1 teaspoon fresh mint, chopped
1 teaspoon fresh basil, chopped
1 green chilli, finely chopped
1 tablespoon oil
salt to taste

For the Thai red curry
½ cup baby corn, halved
¼ cup carrots, diced
½ cup broccoli florets
¼ cup mushrooms, sliced
3 to 4 tablespoons red curry paste, recipe below
1½ cups coconut milk
½ teaspoon soya sauce

Recipe continued on next page

THAI SIZZLER, *recipe above.*

6 to 8 basil leaves, chopped
1 tablespoon cornflour, mixed in ½ cup water
½ tablespoon oil
salt to taste

For the caramelized vegetables
½ cup onions, sliced thickly
1 cup capsicum, cut in to cubes
1 cup zucchini, sliced
½ teaspoon sugar
2 teaspoons oil
salt and pepper to taste

To be ground into a red curry paste
5 red chillies, soaked in warm water for 10 minutes and drained
½ cup onions, chopped
4 cloves garlic, peeled
½ tablespoon ginger, grated
1 stalk lemon grass
½ tablespoon ground coriander (dhania) powder
1 tablespoon ground cumin seeds (jeera)
1 teaspoon white pepper
¼ teaspoon salt

Other ingredients
1 tablespoon oil mixed with 1 tablespoon water

For the sweet corn cutlets
1. Lightly crush the sweet corn in a blender.
2. Add the red curry paste, soya sauce and salt and bind it with the rice flour to make a soft dough.
3. Using lightly oiled hands, shape the mixture into 4 cutlets and deep fry in hot oil till they are golden brown.
4. Drain on absorbent paper. Keep aside.

For the green rice
1. Wash and drain the rice.
2. Heat the oil in a pan, add the rice and fry for 4 to 5 minutes.
3. Add 2 cups of water, the bay leaf and salt and cook on a slow flame, covered with a lid till all the liquid is absorbed.
4. Lower the heat, cover the pan again and cook for 10 minutes or till the rice is done.

5. Remove the bay leaf. Stir in the coriander, mint, basil and green chilli. Keep aside.

For the Thai red curry
1. Parboil the baby corn, carrots, broccoli and mushrooms and keep aside.
2. Heat the oil in a pan, add the red curry paste and saute for a few seconds.
3. Add the coconut milk, soya sauce, basil leaves and all the vegetables and bring to a boil.
4. Add the cornflour paste and salt and simmer for 3 to 5 minutes till the curry thickens. Keep warm.

For the caramelized vegetables
1. Heat the oil in a pan, add the onions and sauté till the onions turn translucent.
2. Add the capsicum and saute for 2 to 3 more minutes. Then add the zucchini slices.
3. Add the sugar, salt and pepper and sauté till the vegetables are caramelized. Keep aside.

How to proceed
1. Heat 2 sizzler plates over an open flame till they are red hot. Then place them on their respective wooden trays.
2. Arrange the caramelized vegetables on the sides of each cast iron plate.
3. Place the warm green rice in the centre and pour the Thai red curry over it.
4. Place 2 hot sweet corn cutlets on one side of the plate.
5. Repeat with the remaining ingredients on the second sizzler plate to make another sizzler.
6. Pour the oil-water mixture over the cast iron plates for a sizzling effect. Serve immediately.

Handy tip : *When you parboil the vegetables for the curry, pour ice cold water over them so that the cooking proces is arrested, resulting in fresh looking vegetables.*

LEBANESE SIZZLER

Simple and sophisticated are two words that come to mind when one thinks of Lebanese cooking. Lebanon is where Arabian cuisine meets the Mediterranean providing the framework for an exotic cuisine that's loved the world over.
This combination comprises of a bed of bean and spinach rice topped with a spicy vegetable curry along with felafel. Serve it with chilled yoghurt spiked with roasted cumin seeds to tone down this fiery sizzler.

Preparation time :
20 minutes.

Cooking time :
45 minutes.

Makes 2 sizzlers.

For the bean and spinach rice
2 cups cooked rice
2 cloves garlic, grated
1 green chilli, finely chopped
1 cup spinach, finely chopped
¼ cup kidney beans (rajma), boiled and cooked
½ teaspoon roasted cumin seed (jeera) powder
1 tablespoon oil
salt to taste

For the vegetables in hot sauce
2 cups boiled vegetables (zucchini, carrots, mushrooms, brinjals), cut into cubes
4 large tomatoes, blanched and peeled
2 teaspoons chilli powder
3 cloves garlic
¼ cup spring onion, whites, finely chopped
½ cup spring onion, greens, finely chopped
½ teaspoon roasted cumin seed (jeera) powder
2 tablespoons tomato ketchup
1 tablespoon oil
salt to taste

For the felafel
1 cup soaked chick peas (kabuli chana)
¼ cup chopped coriander
¼ cup parsley, chopped
½ cup mint (phudina), chopped
1 to 2 green chillies, chopped
2 cloves garlic, chopped

½ teaspoon roasted cumin seed (jeera) powder
salt to taste

Other ingredients
oil for deep frying
2 tablespoons oil mixed with ½ cup water

For the bean and spinach rice
1. Heat the oil in a pan, add the garlic and green chilli and sauté for a few seconds.
2. Add the spinach, kidney beans and salt and sauté for 3 to 4 minutes.
3. Add the rice and cumin seed powder and toss well. Keep aside.

For the vegetables in hot sauce
1. Blend the tomatoes, chilli powder and garlic to a smooth pureé in a blender.
2. Heat the oil in a pan, add the spring onion whites and sauté till they turn translucent.
3. Add the puréed tomatoes, cumin seed powder, tomato ketchup and salt and cook till the oil has separated from the sauce.
4. Add the vegetables and simmer for another 2 to 3 minutes.
5. Add the spring onion greens and mix well. Keep aside.

For the felafel
1. Drain the chick peas. Grind all the ingredients in a blender without using any water to make a coarse paste.
2. Divide the mixture into 4 equal portions and shape each portion into a flat patty.
3. Deep fry the patties in hot oil over a medium flame till they are golden brown in colour.
4. Drain on absorbent paper and keep aside.

How to proceed
1. Heat 2 sizzler plates over an open flame till they are red hot. Then place them on their respective wooden trays.
2. Arrange half of the bean and spinach rice on a hot sizzler plate.
3. Pour half the vegetables in hot sauce over.
4. Place 2 felafels on one side of the sizzler plate.
5. Repeat with the remaining ingredients on the other sizzler plate to make one more sizzler.
6. Pour the oil-water mixture over the cast iron plates for a sizzling effect. Serve immediately.

ITALIAN SIZZLER

Picture on cover

Preparation time :
15 minutes.

Cooking time :
60 minutes.

Makes 2 sizzlers.

Italian cooking is wholesome and flavourful. This sizzler is a hearty combination of pasta tossed in a robust mushroom and black pepper sauce and served with zucchini pancakes. Buttered vegetables and a perfectly baked potato topped with a knob of butter complete this meal.

For the penne with mushroom pepper sauce
2 cups penne pasta, cooked
½ cup onions, sliced
4 cloves garlic, sliced
2 cups mushrooms, sliced
2 sticks celery, cut into 25 mm. (1") pieces
1 tablespoon plain flour (maida)
1 teaspoon coarsely ground pepper
3 tablespoons cream
2 tablespoons oil
salt to taste

For the zucchini pancakes
1 cup zucchini, grated
1 cup carrot, grated
½ cup cottage cheese (paneer), grated
2 to 3 tablespoons plain flour (maida)
½ teaspoon mixed dried herbs
1 teaspoon butter
salt and pepper to taste

For the buttered vegetables
½ cup French beans, cut into strips
½ cup carrots, peeled and cubed
1½ teaspoons butter
salt and pepper to taste

For the baked potatoes
2 medium sized potatoes
2 teaspoons butter
½ teaspoon parsley, chopped
salt and pepper to taste

Other ingredients
butter for cooking the pancakes
1 tablespoon oil mixed with 1 tablespoon water

20

For the penne with mushroom pepper sauce

1. Heat the oil in a pan, add the onions, garlic, mushrooms and celery and sauté till they are browned.
2. Add the flour and sauté for 4 to 5 minutes over a slow flame, till the flour is lightly browned.
3. Add salt and 3 cups of water and simmer till the sauce has thickened (approx. 10 to 15 minutes).
4. Add the pepper and cream and bring the sauce to a boil.
5. Simmer for 2 to 3 minutes and adjust the seasoning. Keep hot.
6. Just before serving, toss the pasta in this sauce and mix well.

For the zucchini pancakes

1. Combine all the ingredients together except the butter and shape into 4 pancakes, 75 mm. (3") in diameter.
2. Cook over a medium flame on a non-stick griddle (tava) using a little butter, till both sides are golden brown. Keep aside.

For the buttered vegetables

1. Parboil all the vegetables and immerse them in cold water.
2. Heat the butter in a pan, add the vegetables, salt and pepper and toss for a few seconds. Keep aside.

For the baked potatoes

1. Apply a little butter on the outer surface of each potato and wrap them separately in pieces of aluminum foil.
2. Bake in a preheated oven at 180°C (350°F) for 45 to 50 minutes or till the potatoes are soft.
3. Slit the potatoes in a criss-cross shape to make a cavity in each and spoon some butter into the cavities.
4. Sprinkle some parsley, salt and pepper on top and keep warm.

How to proceed

1. Heat 2 sizzler plates over an open flame till they are red hot. Place them on their respective wooden trays.
2. Reheat the pasta with the mushroom pepper sauce. Serve half on one side of one sizzler plate.
3. Top with 2 zucchini pancakes on the other side of the sizzler plate.
4. Add some buttered vegetables and one baked potato on the other side of the sizzler plate.
5. Repeat with the remaining ingredients on the other sizzler plate to make another sizzler.
6. Pour the oil-water mixture on the sides of the cast iron plates for a sizzling effect.
   Serve immediately.

MEXICAN SIZZLER

Picture on page 25

Preparation time :
25 minutes.

Cooking time :
60 minutes.

Makes 2 sizzlers.

Let's journey to Mexico..... . The land of tacos and tequila.

This sizzler is a fiery combination of veggie filled tortillas served with a stir-fry and spicy paprika flavoured mashed potatoes.

For the corn tortillas
½ cup maize flour (makai ka atta)
½ cup whole wheat flour (gehun ka atta)
a pinch of salt

For the tortilla filling
¼ cup capsicum, chopped
½ cup onions, chopped
2 large cloves garlic, finely chopped
1 green chilli, finely chopped
¼ cup tomatoes, chopped
¼ cup sweet corn kernels
¼ cup paneer (cottage cheese), chopped
¼ cup baked beans, canned
2 tablespoons spring onion greens, finely chopped
2 teaspoons oil
salt and pepper to taste
2 tablespoons cheese, grated

For the Mexican tomato sauce
1 kg. tomatoes
¾ cup onions, chopped
1 green chilli, chopped
½ teaspoon chilli powder
¼ teaspoon oregano
2 pinches sugar
2 tablespoons oil
salt to taste

For the vegetable stir-fry
½ cup zucchini, sliced
¼ cup carrots, sliced
¼ cup baby corn, sliced
¼ teaspoon roasted cumin seed (jeera) powder
1 teaspoon butter
salt to taste

22

For the paprika mashed potatoes
1 cup boiled and mashed potatoes
1 tablespoon butter
1 to 2 tablespoons milk or cream
½ teaspoon paprika or chilli powder
salt to taste

For the garnish
½ cup spring onions, chopped
¼ cup cheese, grated
½ recipe guacamole, page 68

Other ingredients
1 tablespoon oil mixed with 1 tablespoon water

For the corn tortillas

1. Combine both the flours and salt and knead into a soft dough using warm water.
2. Allow it to rest for 10 to 15 minutes. Divide the dough into 4 equal parts.
3. Roll them into 4 chapatis approx. 150 mm. (6") in diameter.
4. Cook them on a griddle (tava) till both sides are lightly browned. Keep aside.

For the tortilla filling

1. Heat the oil and sauté the capsicum, onions and garlic till the onions are translucent.
2. Add the green chilli, tomatoes, corn, paneer, baked beans, salt and pepper and mix well.
3. Remove from the flame and add the spring onion greens. Add in the cheese and keep aside.

For the Mexican tomato sauce

1. Put the tomatoes in hot water for 10 minutes. Peel the skin and chop the tomatoes.
2. Heat the oil and sauté the onions for ½ minute. Add the green chilli and sauté again for a few seconds.
3. Add the tomatoes, chilli powder, oregano, sugar and salt. Simmer for 10 to 12 minutes till it is thick. Keep aside.

For the vegetable stir-fry

1. Heat the butter in a pan and add the vegetables.
2. Add the salt and ¼ cup of water and allow the vegetables to soften till the water evaporates.
3. Add the cumin powder and mix well.

For the paprika mashed potatoes

1. Combine the milk, butter and salt in a pan and bring to a boil over a slow flame till the butter melts. Add this to the mashed potatoes.
2. Mix all the ingredients in a bowl till the mixture is smooth (strain the mixture if necessary to remove any lumps).
3. Spoon into a piping bag and keep warm.

How to proceed

1. Heat 2 sizzler plates over an open flame till they are red hot and place them on their respective wooden trays.
2. Fill the warm tortillas with the filling mixture and roll them up to make frankie rolls. Keep aside.
3. Place 2 rolls on a hot sizzler plate and surround them with the vegetable stir-fry.
4. Pipe the paprika mashed potatoes on one side of the plate.
5. Pour the Mexican tomato sauce over the tortillas and sprinkle the spring onions and cheese on top. Serve topped with guacamole.
6. Repeat with the remaining ingredients on the other sizzler plate to make another sizzler.
7. Pour the oil-water mixture over the cast iron plates for a sizzling effect. Serve immediately.

MEXICAN SIZZLER, *page 22.*

CONTINENTAL *SIZZLER*

Preparation time :
30 minutes.

Cooking time :
45 minutes.

Makes 2 sizzlers.

Sumptuous cheese corn balls served with buttered parsley rice, glazed vegetables topped with a red wine flavoured tomato sauce. You can serve pasta instead of the rice if you prefer.

For the tomato cream sauce

1½ cups tomatoes, blanched and finely chopped
¼ cup onions, chopped
1 tablespoon garlic, chopped
½ cup red wine (optional)
1 teaspoon chilli flakes
2 tablespoons tomato purée
4 tablespoons fresh cream
2 tablespoons olive oil or oil
salt to taste

For the buttered rice

2 cups cooked rice
½ cup onions, finely chopped
2 tablespoons butter
1 tablespoon parsley, chopped
salt to taste

For the cheese corn balls

¾ cup sweet corn, boiled and crushed
1 heaped tablespoon plain flour (maida)
½ cup milk
1 tablespoon celery, chopped
1 to 2 green chillies, chopped
3 to 4 tablespoons cheese, grated
2 tablespoons butter
salt to taste

Other ingredients (for the cheese corn balls)

¼ cup plain flour (maida) to coat the cheese corn balls
bread crumbs to coat the cheese corn balls
oil for deep frying

For the glazed vegetables

2 onions, cut into thick slices
1 cup mixed boiled vegetables (baby corn, carrots, French beans)
1½ tablespoons butter
salt and pepper to taste

26

Other ingredients
1 tablespoon oil mixed with 1 tablespoon water

For the tomato cream sauce
1. Heat the olive oil, add the garlic and onions and sauté for 1 minute.
2. Add the tomatoes and wine and cook till the sauce thickens.
3. Add the chilli flakes, tomato purée, salt and ½ cup of water and bring to a boil.
4. Add the cream. Mix well and keep aside.

For the buttered rice
1. Heat the butter in a pan, add the onions and sauté for 2 minutes.
2. Add the rice, parsley and salt and toss well.
   Keep aside.

For the cheese corn balls
1. Melt the butter in a pan, add the flour and cook for 1 minute.
2. Add the milk and keep stirring till the mixture becomes very thick and leaves the sides of the pan. Cool completely.
3. Add the crushed corn, celery, green chillies, cheese and salt and mix well.
4. Divide the mixture into 8 equal portions. Shape into even sized balls.
5. Mix ¼ cup of flour with water to make a thin paste. Dip the corn balls into the paste. Roll into breadcrumbs. Keep refrigerated.
6. When you want to serve, deep fry them in oil till they are golden brown. Drain and keep aside.

For the glazed vegetables
1. Heat 1 tablespoon butter in a pan, add the onions, salt and sauté till the onions have turned light brown in colour. Remove and keep aside.
2. Add the vegetables and sauté them over a slow flame for 4 to 7 minutes
3. Add salt and pepper, mix well and keep aside.

How to proceed
1. Heat 2 sizzler plates over an open flame till they are red hot. Then place them on their respective wooden trays.
2. Place half the cheese corn balls on one side of a hot sizzler plate.
3. Place half of the buttered rice in the center of the plate.
4. Top with half the tomato cream sauce and place the caramelized vegetables and onions on the other side.
5. Repeat with the remaining ingredients to make one more sizzler.
6. Pour the oil-water mixture on the sides the cast iron plates for a sizzling effect.
   Serve immediately.

MALPUA RABDI SIZZLER

A mithai lover's delight! Sumptuous malpuas filled with seasonal fruits and topped with creamy rabadi that's made in a jiffy.
You can substitute the seasonal fruits with any one fruit of your choice like mango, strawberries etc. Feel free to serve this dessert without the sizzler plate too. It will be just as delicious, I assure you.

Preparation time :
15 minutes.

Cooking time :
25 minutes.

Makes 2 sizzlers.

For the sugar syrup
½ cup sugar
¼ cup water
a few saffron strands

For the malpuas
1 cup (200 grams) fresh cream
¼ cup plain flour (maida)
½ teaspoon cardamom (elaichi) powder
ghee for cooking

For the malpua stuffing
½ cup chopped mixed fruits (pineapple, peaches, strawberries etc.)
1 teaspoon sugar
1 teaspoon butter

For the rabdi
1½ cups milk
½ cup condensed milk
¼ teaspoon cardamom (elaichi) powder
a few saffron strands

For the skewered fruits
1 cup assorted fruits (pears, apples, oranges, bananas), cut into cubes
1 teaspoon sugar
1 teaspoon melted butter

Other ingredients
2 banana leaves

For the sugar syrup
1. Dissolve the sugar in water and boil for approximately 5 minutes to make a syrup of 1 string consistency.
2. Add the saffron and mix well.
3. Keep the syrup warm.

For the malpuas
1. Combine the cream, plain flour and cardamom powder and mix well to make a smooth batter.
2. Smear very little ghee on a non-stick pan and spread 2 tablespoons of the batter on it to make a 100 mm (4") diameter pancake. Cook on both sides using a little ghee.
3. Repeat with the rest of the batter to make 3 more malpuas.
4. Dip the hot malpuas in the warm syrup for a few seconds. Drain and keep aside.

For the malpua stuffing
Combine all the ingredients in a pan and sauté for a few seconds. Keep aside.

For the rabdi
Combine all the ingredients in a non-stick pan and simmer for 15 to 20 minutes, or until the milk has thickened. Keep aside.

For the skewered fruits
Arrange the fruits on 4 wooden sticks or metallic skewers. Brush with melted butter and sprinkle sugar over them. Keep aside.

How to proceed
1. Lightly heat 2 sizzler plates till they are hot (but not red hot as for other sizzlers) and place them on their respective wooden trays.
2. Place a teaspoon of the stuffing mixture over each malpua and fold into two.
3. Arrange 2 fruit skewers on a hot sizzler plate and place one banana leaf on one side of the hot sizzler plate.
4. Place the stuffed malpuas over the banana leaf on the sizzler plate.
5. Pour half the rabdi over the malpuas.
6. Repeat with the remaining ingredients to make one more sizzler.
   Serve immediately.

Handy tip : *The banana leaf is placed over the sizzler plate to prevent the malpuas and rabdi from getting scorched.*

SIZZLING BROWNIES

Picture on facing page

Preparation time :
15 minutes.

Cooking time :
60 minutes.

Makes 2 brownies.

A rich, gooey, sinful and truly indulgent dessert. Warm, fudgy walnut brownies served with rum marinated fruits, drizzled with chocolate sauce that is streaked with fresh cream. And what is a brownie served without the mandatory scoop of vanilla ice-cream. So dig in and indulge.

For the brownies
1 cup plain flour (maida)
¼ cup cocoa powder
¾ cup powdered sugar
½ teaspoon soda bi-carb
½ teaspoon baking powder
6 tablespoons curds
5 tablespoons milk
5 tablespoons melted butter
½ cup chopped walnuts
½ teaspoon vanilla essence

To be mixed together for the marinated fruits
1½ cups mixed fruits (strawberries, grapes, cherries etc.)
1 tablespoon rum
1 teaspoon castor sugar
½ teaspoon lemon juice (optional)
½ teaspoon lemon rind

For the marbled chocolate sauce
1½ cups grated dark chocolate
½ cup cream

Recipe continued on next page

SIZZLING BROWNIES, *recipe above.*

Other ingredients
2 scoops of vanilla ice-cream

For the brownies
1. Pre-heat the oven to 180 C (350 F).
2. Mix all the ingredients in a mixing bowl using a wooden spoon, making sure there are no lumps.
3. Pour this mixture into a greased and dusted 200 mm. x 200 mm. (8" x 8") baking tray.
4. Place in the oven and bake for 20 to 25 minutes.
5. Cool and cut into 50 mm. x 50 mm. (2" x 2") pieces. Keep aside.

For the marbled chocolate sauce
1. Keep aside 2 tablespoons of the cream and pour the rest into a pan. Bring it to a boil and remove from the fire.
2. Add the chocolate and mix well till it is of a sauce like consistency. Keep aside.

How to proceed
1. Lightly heat 2 sizzler plates till they are hot (but not red hot as for other sizzlers) and place them on their respective wooden trays.
2. Pour some of the chocolate sauce over 1 sizzler plate and drizzle some fresh cream over.
3. Using a toothpick, streak the cream into the chocolate sauce to create a marbled effect.
4. Place half the brownies and then the marinated fruits on the sides. (Reheat the brownies if cold).
5. Serve hot with a scoop of vanilla ice-cream and the chocolate sauce.
6. Repeat with the remaining ingredients to make another sizzler. Serve immediately.

Handy tip : *If you like, soak the brownies with some rum before you place them on the sizzler platter.*

CARROT PANCAKE SIZZLER

Gajar ka halwa filled into crêpes and served with rabdi. These are served on a bed of pineapple slices so that the delicate crêpes do not burn and the pineapple slices are lightly grilled on the sizzler plate adding more flavour to this tantalizing dessert.

Preparation time :
20 minutes.

Cooking time :
40 minutes.

Makes 2 sizzlers.

For the crêpes
¼ cup plain flour (maida)
¼ cup cornflour
⅓ cup milk
1 teaspoon melted butter
a pinch of salt

For the carrot halwa
¾ cup carrots, grated
¼ cup full fat milk
2 tablespoons castor sugar
a pinch cardamom (elaichi) powder
a few saffron strands
2 teaspoons milk powder
1 teaspoon ghee

For the rabdi
1½ cups milk
½ cup condensed milk
¼ teaspoon cardamom (elaichi) powder
a few saffron strands

Other ingredients
4 thin pineapple slices, canned
2 edible silver leaves (varq)
2 tablespoons slivered pistachios

For the crêpes
1. Mix the plain flour, cornflour, milk, salt and ¼ cup of water. Mix very well until no lumps remain.
2. Grease a 125 mm. (5") diameter non-stick pan with the butter.
3. Pour 2 tablespoons of the batter, tilt the pan around quickly so that the batter coats the pan evenly.
4. When the sides start to peel off, turn the pancake around and cook the other side for 30 seconds.

5. Repeat with the remaining batter, greasing the pan with butter when required.
   Keep aside.
6. You can make these crêpes ahead of time and store them refrigerated, wrapped in plastic film.

For the carrot halwa
1. Dissolve the saffron in a little warm milk. Keep aside.
2. Heat the ghee in a pan and sauté the carrots for a few minutes till they soften.
3. Add the milk and sugar and simmer till the milk is absorbed.
4. Add the cardamom powder, saffron and milk powder and mix well. Keep aside.

For the rabdi
Combine all the ingredients in a non-stick pan and simmer for 15 to 20 minutes or until the milk has reduced to half the original quantity at least. Keep aside.

How to proceed
1. Divide the carrot halwa into four equal portions.
2. Put one portion of the halwa on each pancake and roll them.
3. Lightly heat two sizzler plates till they are hot (but not red hot as for the other sizzlers).
4. Place 2 slices of pineapple in the center of one sizzler plate.
5. Arrange 2 pancake rolls on top.
6. Pour half the rabdi over the pancakes.
7. Garnish with varq and pistachios.
8. Repeat with the remaining ingredients to make one more sizzler.
   Serve immediately.

FRUIT & ICE-CREAM SIZZLER

Barbequed butterey bananas, served with brandy marinated fruits that are served with vanilla ice-cream. Add a dollop of chocolate sauce if you like.

For the barbequed bananas
2 bananas
2 tablespoons brown sugar
2 tablespoons butter, softened

For the marinated fruits
2 cups assorted cut fruits (pears, apple, pomegranate seeds, peaches etc.)
1 cup orange juice
2 tablespoons orange squash
¼ cup brown sugar
2 teaspoons cornflour
½ teaspoon lemon juice
3 tablespoons brandy

Other ingredients
2 to 4 scoops of vanilla ice-cream

Preparation time :
20 minutes.

Cooking time :
5 minutes.

Makes 2 sizzlers.

For the barbequed bananas
1. Cut the bananas lengthwise and keep aside.
2. Combine the brown sugar and butter and apply it generously over the bananas. Keep aside.

For the marinated fruits
Combine all the ingredients and keep aside for about one hour.

How to proceed
1. Heat 2 sizzler plates till they are red hot and place them on their respective wooden trays.
2. Place one banana piece on each side of a hot sizzler plate. Allow the pieces to char slightly.
3. Turn the banana pieces so as to grill the other side as well.
4. Pour half the portion of the marinated fruits in the centre of the plate and stir with a spoon so that the fruits sizzle a bit and the cornflour in the sauce cooks.
5. Serve immediately topped with scoops of vanilla ice-cream.
Repeat with the remaining ingredients to make one more sizzler.

Barbeques
& Grills

Barbequing and grilling vegetables is easy, the fact that more people don't do it is really strange.!!

Barbequed or grilled vegetables fully absorb the flavours they have been marinated or cooked with. They are lightly charred on the outside but still retain the wonderful tenderness inside.
You can either use an electric barbeque or a charcoal one to grill these smoky delicacies and on a lazy day, feel free to toss them in a nonstick pan and make as unusual stir-fry of sorts...... !

Start out with the freshest, recently picked foods. Most fruits and vegetables benefit from basting or a light brushing with a marinade, butter, or oil. Alternately, try any of .... these 23 sumptuous ways to prepare them and enjoy these delectable morsels in your meal....

Turn over for a few pointers on some finer points about barbequing and grilling.

Once you've made the decision of whether to use an electric barbeque or a charcoal one, out of the way, you are all set to begin. If you're using an electric barbeque or grill, simply follow the instruction manual to the 'T'. However if you're going to be doing it the old-fashioned way, you do have a few options to consider...wood fired or charcoal fired being among the first few decisions to make.

Use wood or coal, whichever you prefer or is easily available. Light one piece of wood or charcoal till it is red-hot and then place it with the remaining coal or wood in the barbeque pit. Fan this lightly, in order to ignite the remaining wood or coal. A mass of glowing embers will indicate the readiness of the wood, however, charcoal is only ready when it is grayish-white.

Remember to avoid using either petroleum or kerosene as a starter to ignite the barbeque, as it will impart a peculiar, unpleasant odour to the food.

BEFORE YOU BEGIN

✓ Keep the grill clean. Oil regarlarly and scrub the rack with a wire brush in between consecutive grillings. Charred buildup is unhealthy and encourages food to stick.
✓ Clean the grill by covering it with a sheet of aluminum foil, shiny side down and heating the grill for ten to fifteen minutes. The muck on the grill will drop right off!!
✓ Heat the cooking grid and apply cold vegetable oil to it using a long-handle, brush to help prevent food from sticking,
✓ Watch out for flame-ups resulting from the oil dripping onto the fire.
✓ Keep a spritzer bottle with a 4 to 1 mixture of water and baking soda handy, in case you need to douse flare-ups.

COOKING

✓ The general rules are to cut the vegetables into pieces that will cook quickly and evenly. All pieces should be of consistent thickness of no more than about 3/4 to 1 inch thick.
✓ Fast-cooking foods, such as tomato slices, do best over a hot fire, while others, such as potatoes and onions, require to be grilled for longer periods over medium heat. Especially slow-cooking vegetables, like fennel grill best after longer marination.
✓ Grill vegetables and fruits just until the outsides are golden for by then they would have achieved the desirable tenderness inside.
✓ Vegetables like potatoes, onions, eggplant, leeks, peppers, and cauliflower benefit from 10 minutes of steaming prior to grilling if you want to shorten their cooking time. After precooking, they'll need as little as 8 to 12 minutes on the grill.

Grilled Mediterranean Mushrooms

A treat for mushroom lovers! Cheese, olives and garlic filled mushrooms makes an easy to assemble dish that is perfect for an outdoor party. They also make an innovative side dish to a main course like pasta.

Preparation time :
15 minutes.

Cooking time :
10 minutes.

Makes 12 pieces.

12 large button mushrooms

To be mixed into a filling
1 tablespoon onions, finely chopped
2 tablespoons olives, finely chopped
¼ cup mushroom stalks, finely chopped
½ teaspoon garlic, finely chopped
1 tablespoon celery, finely chopped
2 tablespoons grated cheese
a pinch mixed dried herbs
salt and pepper to taste
1 teaspoon butter

Other ingredients
1 tablespoon melted butter

1. Carefully remove the stalks from the mushrooms and keep the caps aside.
2. Chop the stalks finely and combine them with the filling ingredients. Use the remaining stalks to make a sauce or a stock.
3. Carefully spoon the filling mixture into the mushrooms ensuring that they do not break.
4. Thread them on to 3 skewers and brush with a little melted butter.
5. Grill them over a charcoal or electric barbeque for 10 minutes or till the mushrooms are cooked and the cheese has melted.
 Serve hot.

Handy tip : *You can sauté the onions, olives, mushrooms stalks, garlic and celery in a little olive oil and then combine it with the cheese if you prefer. Then fill it in the mushrooms before you proceed to grill them.*

Barbequed Mushrooms and Peas

Mushrooms and peas in a delectable barbeque sauce.

2 cups mushrooms, washed
½ cup green peas, boiled
½ recipe barbeque sauce, page 71
1 teaspoon melted butter
1 teaspoon cornflour
salt and pepper to taste

Preparation time :
15 minutes.

Cooking time :
30 minutes.

Serves 4.

1. Grease the mushrooms with some melted butter, thread them onto a skewer and grill over a charcoal or electric barbeque for 10 to 12 minutes or until the mushrooms are cooked.
2. Mix together the mushrooms, peas and all the ingredients and leave aside for 15 minutes.
3. Wrap in a foil wrapper and grill them over a charcoal or electric barbeque for 10 to 15 minutes.
4. Carefully unwrap the foil wrapper allowing the steam to escape. Serve hot.

Handy tip : *You can also sauté the ingredients in a pan instead of grilling them.*

Cheesy Broccoli Stuffed Mushrooms

Picture on facing page

This in one of my favourite ways of cooking mushrooms. Mushrooms take readily to grilling and the cheesy broccoli filling enhances the natural flavours of mushrooms instead of masking it as most other mushroom dishes do. Simple, clean flavours that are sure to appeal.

Preparation time :
15 minutes.

Cooking time :
10 minutes.

Makes 12 pieces.

12 large button mushrooms
1 teaspoon melted butter for greasing

For the filling
1 tablespoon onion, finely chopped
½ teaspoon garlic, finely chopped
½ cup broccoli florets, grated
2 tablespoons cheese, grated
½ teaspoon green chilli, finely chopped
salt to taste
2 teaspoons butter

For serving
barbeque sauce, page 71

For the filling
1. Heat 1 teaspoon of butter in a pan and sauté the onion and garlic for 2 to 3 minutes.
2. Add the grated broccoli and salt and sauté over a medium flame till the broccoli softens.
3. Remove from the flame, add the cheese and green chilli and mix well.

Recipe continued on next page

1. **PUDINA ALOO,** *page 53.*
2. **SPICY BABY CORN,** *page 52.*
3. **CORN ON THE COB,** *page 60.*
4. **COTTAGE CHEESE CUTLETS,** *page 49.*
5. **CHEESY BROCCOLI STUFFED MUSHROOMS,** *recipe above.*

How to proceed

1. Carefully remove the stalks from the mushrooms and keep the caps aside. Use the mushroom stalks to make a sauce or a stock.
2. Carefully spoon the filling mixture into the mushrooms ensuring that they do not break.
3. Thread them on to 3 skewers and grease them with a little melted butter.
4. Grill them over a medium flame for 10 minutes or till the mushrooms are cooked and the cheese has melted.
   Serve hot with barbeque sauce, page 71.

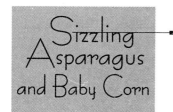

Tender asparagus and baby corn topped with a paprika flavoured cheese sauce. It makes an interesting starter to serve with aperitifs.

8 to 10 asparagus, cut into 25 mm. (1") pieces and blanched
8 to 10 baby corn, cut into 25 mm. (1") pieces and blanched

Preparation time :
10 minutes.

Cooking time :
15 minutes.

Serves 4.

For the cheese sauce
1 teaspoon garlic, finely chopped
4 to 6 cheese slices
½ teaspoon oregano
¼ cup cream
¼ cup milk
1 teaspoon chilli flakes
2 tablespoons butter
salt to taste

For the garnish
1 teaspoon chopped parsley

For the cheese sauce

1. Heat the butter in a non-stick pan, add the garlic and sauté for a few seconds.
2. Add the cheese, oregano, cream, milk, chilli flakes and salt and stir over a slow flame till the cheese has melted to get a smooth cheese sauce.

42

How to proceed

1. Heat one small sizzler plate till it is red hot and place it on its wooden tray.
2. Arrange the asparagus and baby corn pieces over the hot sizzler plate.
3. Pour the cheese sauce over.
   Serve immediately, garnished with the parsley.

Succulent cubes of paneer, marinated in an oriental honey chilli marinade and grilled till the honey just about caramelizes, imparting an unusual flavour to this dish.

1 cup paneer (cottage cheese), cut into 25 mm. (1") cubes
4 spring onions (including greens), finely chopped
2 tablespoons honey
1 tablespoon chilli sauce
1 teaspoon lemon juice
¼ teaspoon lemon rind
3 cloves garlic, grated
1 tablespoon chopped coriander
1 tablespoon oil
salt to taste

Preparation time :
15 minutes.

Cooking time :
10 minutes.

Serves 2.

1. Combine all the ingredients in a bowl and mix well. Allow to marinate for at least 15 minutes.
2. Arrange the paneer cubes neatly onto 4 wooden skewers and grill them over a charcoal or electric barbeque till they are lightly browned on all sides. Serve hot.

Sizzling Mushrooms in Salsa

Mushrooms tossed in a fiery salsa makes a super appetizer or can even be used a pasta sauce if it is thinned down with a little wine and cream.

1 cup mushrooms, cut into quarters
2 tablespoons tomato ketchup
¼ cup spring onion greens, finely chopped

For the cooked salsa
2 large cloves garlic, finely chopped
1 green chilli, finely chopped
¼ cup spring onions whites, finely chopped
¼ cup capsicum, finely chopped
½ cup tomatoes, finely chopped
¼ teaspoon oregano
2 tablespoons oil
salt to taste

For the garnish
¼ cup grated cheese
1 tablespoon cream

Preparation time :
10 minutes.

Cooking time :
15 minutes.

Serves 2.

For the cooked salsa
1. Heat the oil in a pan, add the garlic, green chilli, spring onion whites and capsicum and sauté for 3 to 4 minutes.
2. Add the tomatoes and sauté for 2 to 3 minutes. Keep aside.

How to proceed
1. Add the tomato ketchup, mushrooms and salt to the cooked salsa and sauté for 3 to 4 minutes till the mushrooms soften.
2. Add the spring onion greens and oregano and mix well.
3. Spoon the mushrooms on to a hot sizzler plate.
   Serve immediately topped with the cheese and cream.

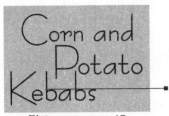

Corn and Potato Kebabs

Picture on page 47

Preparation time :
10 minutes.

Cooking time :
15 minutes.

Makes 4 kebabs.

A simple and subtle blend of ingredients shaped on a skewer and grilled to create seekh kebabs... of a vegetarian kind. You can even shape them into tikkis and shallow fry if you like.

1 cup sweet corn, boiled
1 cup potato, boiled and grated
2 tablespoons chopped coriander
2 green chillies, finely chopped
¼ teaspoon garam masala
2 teaspoons lemon juice
2 to 3 tablespoons bread crumbs
salt to taste

Other ingredients
oil for grilling

For serving
green chutney, page 67

1. Combine all the ingredients in a bowl and mix well.
2. Divide the mixture into 4 equal portions.
3. Using a thick seekh (metal skewer), press each portion of the corn mixture on it using your fingers to make a 100 mm. (4") long kebab.
4. Brush each kebab generously with a little oil.
5. Cook the kebabs over a charcoal or electric barbeque till the kebabs are evenly browned (approx. 3 to 4 minutes), on all sides.
6. Cut into pieces and serve hot with green chutney.

Handy tip : *If you do not have metal skewers use thin breadsticks instead. The will make interesting edible skewers.*

Grilled Pepper Bruschetta

Bruschettas are of Italian origin and are traditionally prepared by grilling a toast over a wood fire in order to infuse the smoky taste. I have however, used a charcoal barbeque for making these you can also use the electric one if you like or even an oven will do just as well.

Preparation time :
10 minutes.

Cooking time :
10 minutes.

Makes 6.

6 slices French bread (approx. ¾" thick)
1 clove garlic, grated
1 tablespoon butter

For the topping
2 tablespoons onions, chopped
¼ cup red or yellow peppers, finely chopped
¼ teaspoon oregano
3 tablespoons mozzarella or cooking cheese, grated
1 teaspoon butter
salt to taste

For the topping
1. Heat the olive oil in a pan, add the onions and peppers and sauté for a few minutes till they are lightly browned.
2. Add the oregano and salt and mix well.
3. Cool, add the cheese and mix again.

How to proceed
1. Cream the butter and garlic together and keep aside.
2. Apply some garlic butter onto each bread slice and grill over a charcoal or electric barbeque for 2 to 3 minutes on both sides.
3. Spoon the topping mixture on to each slice and grill over a slow charcoal or electric barbeque for another 2 to 3 minutes until the cheese has melted. Serve hot.

1. MOONG DAL SEEKH KEBABS, *page 50.*
2. CORN AND POTATO KEBABS, *page 45.*
3. SURAN CHANA DAL SEEKH KEBABS, *page 51.*

Tandoori Gobi Aur Broccoli

Picture on page 57

This popular marinade has always been a mystery to most of us who enjoy its piquant blend of spices. Cauliflower and broccoli are smothered in this delectable marinade and grilled. If you like, you can also use paneer instead.

Preparation time :
1 hour.

Cooking time :
20 minutes.

Serves 4.

1 cup cauliflower florets, parboiled
1 cup broccoli florets, parboiled

To be mixed into a marinade
½ cup thick curds
1 teaspoon Bengal gram flour (besan)
1 teaspoon chilli powder
1 teaspoon roasted cumin seed (jeera) powder
2 teaspoons ginger-garlic paste
½ teaspoon kasuri methi (dried fenugreek leaves)
2 teaspoons chaat masala
2 tablespoons chopped coriander
1 tablespoon mustard oil or oil
salt to taste

For serving
onion rings
mint leaves

1. Marinate the cauliflower and broccoli florets in the prepared marinade for about 1 hour.
2. Thread them on to skewers.
3. Grill the marinated cauliflower and broccoli florets over a charcoal or electric barbeque till the cauliflower is tender (approx. 15 to 20 minutes). Serve hot on a bed of onion rings and mint leaves.

Cottage Cheese Cutlets

Picture on page 41

This is not really a barbeque recipe but I like the way the cottage cheese melts lightly when grilled just before you serve them. It's also a substantial dish to add to a barbeque menu. Serve them with burger buns to make veggie burgers.

Preparation time :
25 minutes.

Cooking time :
30 minutes.

Makes 4 cutlets.

1 cup potatoes, boiled and mashed
1 cup cottage cheese (paneer), grated
2 tablespoons chopped coriander
4 to 6 green chillies, chopped
½ cup onions, chopped
1 cup cabbage, finely chopped
3 slices bread
salt to taste

Other ingredients
1 cup plain flour (maida)
bread crumbs
oil for deep frying

1. Soak the bread slices in water for 2 minutes and then squeeze out the water.
2. Combine the potatoes, cheese, coriander, chillies, onions, cabbage, bread slices and salt and mix well.
3. Shape into 4 cutlets.
4. Mix the flour in 1 cup of water to make a smooth batter. Dip the cutlets in this paste and roll into bread crumbs.
5. Deep fry in oil, drain on absorbent paper and keep aside.
6. Just before you wish to serve, grill them over a charcoal or electric barbeque. Serve hot with the barbeque sauce, page 71.

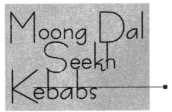

Picture on page 47

This is a vegetarian version of the non-vegetarian seekh kebabs.

Moong dal when combined with potatoes and onions tastes simply superb. Dip these kebabs in your favourite sauce or chutney. Alternatively, serve them wrapped in rotis to make kebab rolls, a more filling snack.

Preparation time :
10 minutes.

Cooking time :
1 minutes.

Makes 4 kebabs.

1 cup yellow moong dal (split yellow gram)
1 cup boiled potato, grated
3 tablespoons grated onions
2 teaspoons chilli powder
¼ teaspoon garam masala
¼ teaspoon turmeric powder (haldi)
1 teaspoon ginger-garlic paste
2 teaspoons chaat masala
2 tablespoons chopped coriander
salt to taste

Other ingredients
oil for grilling

1. Clean, wash and boil the moong dal in 1 cup of water till the dal is soft and cooked and all the water has evaporated.
2. Combine the cooked dal with the rest of the ingredients and mix well.
3. Divide the mixture into 4 equal portions.
4. Using a thick seekh (metal skewer), press each portion of the dal mixture on it using your fingers to make a 100 mm. (4") long kebab.
5. Brush each kebab with oil.
6. Cook the kebabs over a charcoal or electric barbeque till they are evenly browned (approx. 3 to 4 minutes) on all sides.
6. Cut into pieces and serve hot with green chutney, page 67.

Suran Chana Dal Seekh Kebabs

Picture on page 47

An unusual combination of flavours and ingredients creates a sumptuous snack that is sure to tickle your taste buds.
Makes a great burger filling too.

Preparation time :
15 minutes.

Cooking time :
1 hour.

Makes 4 kebabs.

½ cup split Bengal gram (chana dal)
1½ cups suran (yam), finely chopped
½ cup onions, sliced
1½ teaspoons grated ginger
2 cloves garlic, chopped
2 green chillies, chopped
¼ cup chopped mint (phudina)
1 tablespoon chaat masala
¼ teaspoon garam masala
3 tablespoons oil
salt to taste
oil for grilling

For serving
green chutney, page 67
onion rings

1. Heat 1 tablespoon of oil in a pan, add the chana dal and sauté it till it is light pink in colour.
2. Cool and grind the chana dal to a powder. Keep aside.
3. In another pan, heat the remaining 2 tablespoons of oil and sauté the onions, ginger, garlic and green chillies till the onions turn translucent.
4. Add the suran and cook over a slow flame for 5 to 7 minutes. Add ½ cup of water and cover and cook till the suran is soft and all the moisture has evaporated.
5. Cool and grind to a paste along with the mint without using any water.
6. Combine the chana dal powder, suran mixture, chaat masala, garam masala and salt and mix well.
7. Divide into 4 equal portions and shape them into kebabs on metal skewers that are 100 mm. (4") long.
8. Brush each kebab with a little oil.
9. Grill over a charcoal or electric barbeque till they are lightly browned on all sides.
Serve hot with green chutney, page 67, and onion rings.

Spicy Baby Corn

Picture on page 41

A tempting blend of spices is used to marinate baby corn in this recipe..... feel free to use any other ingredients of your choice in place of the baby corn.

Preparation time :
10 minutes.

Cooking time :
15 minutes.

Serves 4.

200 grams baby corn

To be mixed into a marinade
1 teaspoon chilli powder
1 teaspoon garlic, grated
¼ teaspoon ajwain (carom seeds)
1 teaspoon oil
1 teaspoon cornflour
3 tablespoon curds
salt to taste

For serving
½ cup spring onions, chopped
lemon wedges
spring onion and curd dip, page 72

1. Combine the marinade with the baby corn and leave aside for 15 to 20 minutes.
2. Grill over a charcoal or electric barbeque, either by wrapping in foil or by threading onto skewers.
3. Grill over a slow flame till the corn is almost cooked and the marinade is cooked and has coated the corn.
4. Arrange on a bed of spring onions and lemon wedges and serve with the spring onion and curd dip, page 72.

Pudina Aloo

Spicy mint flavoured potatoes wrapped in foil and grilled so that they remain moist.
If you like them lightly browned, feel free to thread the potatoes on a skewer, grill them.

Picture on page 41

Preparation time :
10 minutes.

Cooking time :
15 minutes.

Serves 4.

2 cups baby potatoes
½ recipe green chutney, page 67
¼ teaspoon black salt (sanchal)
1 tablespoon melted butter
1½ teaspoons cornflour
salt to taste

1. Boil the potatoes in salted water and peel them.
2. Combine all the ingredients together in a bowl and keep aside for 10 minutes.
3. Place the potatoes in a foil wrapper and grill over a medium hot barbeque (charcoal or electric) for 10 to 12 minutes till the cornflour is cooked and the marinade coats the potatoes.
Serve hot.

Handy tip : *You can also pierce the potatoes with a fork before you boil them so that when you marinate them, the marinade is absorbed in the potatoes.*

Kand Aur Shimla Mirch

Yam and capsicum smeared with cumin flavoured butter and grilled. You can even toss them in a non-stick pan if you are not up to barbequing them.

Picture on page 57

Preparation time :
10 minutes.

Cooking time :
10 minutes.

Serves 4.

1½ cups kand (purple yam), boiled and cubed
1 cup capsicum, cubed
1 teaspoon roasted cumin (jeera) powder
2 tablespoons melted butter
salt to taste

For serving
½ teaspoon chilli powder
1 to 2 teaspoons lemon juice
spring onion and curd dip, page 72

1. Combine all the ingredients in a bowl and mix well.
2. Thread the kand and capsicum onto skewers and grill them over a charcoal or electric barbeque till they are lightly browned.
3. Sprinkle with the chilli powder and lemon juice.
   Serve hot with the spring onion and curd dip, page 72.

Basil Grilled Tomatoes and Onions

Picture on page 57

A touch of the Mediterrenean on your barbeque. Basil and garlic complement tomatoes beautifully to create this simple but stunning dish. Select firm and ripe tomatoes for best results.

Preparation time :
10 minutes.

Cooking time :
15 minutes.

Makes 4 kebabs.

12 cherry tomatoes
1 onion, cut into 12 (12 mm. (½") wedges

To be mixed into a marinade
2 tablespoons olive oil
1 teaspoon chopped fresh basil
1 large clove garlic, grated
salt and pepper to taste

1. Pierce the tomatoes in 1 to 2 places using a fork and then place them in the marinade along with the onions wedges. Allow to marinate for about 30 minutes.
2. Thread the onion and tomatoes alternately on skewers draining out and keeping aside the excess marinade that remains.
3. Grill the skewers over a barbeque for 5 to 7 minutes till the tomatoes and onions are lightly browned. Drizzle some of the marinade while you grill them.
   Serve hot with garlic bread.

Handy tip : *You can also use this marinade as an interesting salad dressing.*

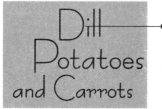

Dill Potatoes and Carrots

Picture on page 57

Dill is not a herb we use on a daily basis but if it is used judiciously, can create a subtle blend of flavours that are guaranteed to please. Carrots and potatoes are vegetables that absorb the flavours beautifully.

Preparation time :
10 minutes.

Cooking time :
20 minutes.

Serves 4.

10 to 12 baby potatoes
1 to 2 carrots, peeled and thickly sliced
2 tablespoons melted butter
1 teaspoon chopped dill (suva bhaji)
salt and pepper to taste

To serve
lemon wedges

1. Boil the potatoes and carrots in salted water. Peel the potatoes and keep aside.
2. Combine the butter, dill, salt and pepper and mix well.
3. Toss the potatoes and carrots and mix well so that the butter coats the potatoes and carrots.
4. Thread them alternatively onto 4 skewers and grill them over a charcoal or electric barbeque till they are lightly browned.
   Serve hot with lemon wedges.

1. TANDOORI GOBI AUR BROCCOLI, *page 48.*
2. KAND AUR SHIMLA MIRCH, *page 54.*
3. BASIL GRILLED TOMATOES AND ONIONS, *page 55.*
4. DILL POTATOES AND CARROTS, *recipe above.*

Cheesy Spinach Parcels

These melt in the mouth dainty cheese filled spinach parcels are cooked in garlic flavoured butter. Use whole spinach leaves that do not have any cracks because the cheese can ooze out of the leaves during cooking.

Preparation time :
10 minutes.

Cooking time :
20 minutes.

Serves 4.

For the spinach parcels
12 large spinach leaves
½ cup cheese
freshly crushed pepper to taste

To be mixed into a garlic butter
1 tablespoon melted butter
1 teaspoon garlic, grated

1. Using a pair of chapati tongs, immerse each spinach leaf in hot water for a few seconds.
2. Refresh each leaf in ice-cold water and dry carefully on a cotton towel or napkin.
3. Place the spinach leaves flat on a dry surface.
4. Place 1 teaspoon of the cheese on one corner of the leaf and sprinkle some pepper over it.
5. Roll the spinach leaf into a parcel, sealing the cheese securely in the leaf.
6. Repeat with the remaining ingredients to make more spinach parcels.
7. Thread them on 4 wooden skewers and barbeque on a medium flame over a charcoal or an electric barbeque. Drizzle with some of the garlic butter while they are being grilled and serve immediately.

Grilled Curry Rice

An aromatic rice preparation steamed in a banana leaf. This is a perfect meal to go with all the great starters that you make on your barbeque.

3 cups cooked rice
½ cup coconut milk
2 to 3 teaspoons red curry paste, page 16
½ cup mixed boiled vegetables
½ teaspoon lemon rind, grated
1 tablespoon basil leaves, finely chopped
1 large banana leaf
salt to taste

Preparation time :
15 minutes.

Cooking time :
15 minutes.

Serves 4.

1. Mix the coconut milk and red curry paste in a bowl.
2. Add the mixed vegetables and mix well. Add the lemon rind, basil leaves and salt and mix well.
3. Add the rice, stirring until thoroughly mixed.
4. Spoon this flavoured rice onto the centre of a banana leaf (kitchen foil can be used as substitute).
5. Fold the leaf into a square packets and tie using a string. Grill on a charcoal grill or an electric barbeque turning over from time to time until steam comes out.
   Serve hot.

Handy tip : *This recipe makes good use of left-over rice.*

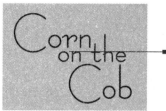

Corn on the Cob

Picture on page 41

Preparation time :
5 minutes.

Cooking time :
15 minutes.

Makes 2 cobs.

Sweet corn cobs smothered with cumin flavoured butter makes a wholesome addition to any meal. It also makes a delicious snack all by itself.

2 sweet corn cobs

To be mixed together for the cumin-coriander butter
1 tablespoon chopped coriander
1 teaspoon roasted cumin seed (jeera) powder
1 teaspoon lemon juice (optional)
2 tablespoons melted butter
salt to taste

1. Clean the corn cobs and trim the stems. Cut into 50 mm. (2") pieces.
2. Roast the cobs over a charcoal or an electric barbeque till they are lightly browned.
3. Brush the flavoured butter on the cobs.
   Serve hot.

Handy tip : *If you like, you can even boil the corn cobs instead of grilling them and serve drizzled with the flavoured butter.*

Tandoori Aloo aur Baby Corn

This is one of my favourite recipes. I store the marinade in the refrigerator to whip up this snack whenever unexpected guests arrive.

Preparation time :
5 minutes.

Cooking time :
20 minutes.

Serves 4.

1 cup baby potatoes
1 cup baby corn, cut into 25 mm. (1") pieces and blanched
3 tablespoon cream
½ teaspoon kasuri methi (dried fenugreek leaves)
1 tablespoon mustard oil
salt to taste

To be ground into a paste
6 to 8 Kashmiri chillies
4 cloves garlic
25 mm. (1") piece ginger
4 teaspoons coriander-cumin seed (dhania-jeera) powder

For serving
lemon wedges
onion rings

1. Wash the potatoes thoroughly, pierce them with a fork and boil in salted water till they are done.
2. Make a marinade by combining the ground paste, cream, kasuri methi, mustard oil and salt.
3. Marinate the potatoes and baby corn in this marinade for 10 to 15 minutes.
4. Arrange alternate pieces of potatoes and baby corn on skewers.
5. Grill over a charcoal or electric barbeque till they are golden brown.
   Serve hot with lemon wedges and onion rings.

Aloo Shakarkand Ke Kebab

This dish is almost a meal in itself. Potatoes and sweet potatoes are grilled with butter, then topped with curds and spices and garnished with grated radish and spring onions.

Preparation time :
10 minutes.

Cooking time :
30 minutes.

Serves 4.

2 large potatoes
2 medium sweet potatoes (shakarkand)
4 tablespoons green chutney, page 67
½ cup khajur imli ki chutney, page 69
1 cup fresh curds, beaten
¼ teaspoon black salt (sanchal)
½ teaspoon roasted cumin seed (jeera) powder
¼ teaspoon chilli powder
4 tablespoons melted butter
salt to taste

For the garnish
½ cup grated white radish (mooli)
½ cup spring onions, chopped

1. Boil the potatoes and sweet potatoes in salted water. Peel and cut into large cubes.
2. Thread the potato and sweet potato cubes onto skewers. Smear them generously with melted butter and grill over a charcoal or electric barbecue till they are golden brown.
3. Drain on absorbent paper and place in a serving dish.
4. Top with the green chutney, khajur imli ki chutney, curds, black salt, cumin seed powder, chilli powder and salt.
5. Garnish with the grated radish and spring onions.
   Serve immediately

BARBEQUED PINEAPPLE SLICES, *page 64.*

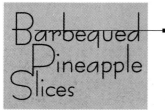

Barbequed Pineapple Slices

Picture on page 63

Fresh pineapple slices grilled with butter, cinnamon and brown sugar. Flambéeing them with rum or brandy makes a befitting finale to a colourful barbeque and definitely adds more life to this dessert.

Preparation time :
15 minutes.

Cooking time :
10 minutes.

Serves 4.

8 pineapple slices
3 tablespoons butter
2 tablespoons brown sugar
¼ teaspoon cinnamon (dalchini) powder
1 tablespoon brandy or rum (optional)

For serving
vanilla ice-cream

1. Combine the butter, brown sugar and cinnamon in a bowl and cream the mixture till it is soft and creamy.
2. Using a knife, spread an even layer of the creamed butter mixture on both sides of each pineapple slice.
3. Grill the pineapple slices on both sides over a charcoal or electric barbeque till they are lightly browned.
4. Pour the brandy in a ladle and warm it lightly. Pour over the pineapples and set it alight, allowing them to get flambéed.
   Serve immediately with a scoop of vanilla ice-cream.

VARIATION : *You can also use bananas with the same marinade.*

Sauces & Dips

Chilli Garlic Chutney

10 red Kashmiri chillies
10 to 12 garlic cloves
1 teaspoon lemon juice
salt to taste

Preparation time :
20 minutes.

No Cooking.

Makes ¼ cup.

1. Soak the chillies in ½ cup of warm water for at least 15 minutes till they soften. Drain and keep aside. Remove the seeds if you do not want a spicy chutney.
2. Grind the chillies and garlic with ½ cup of water along with the lemon juice and salt. Store refrigerated in an airtight container.

Green Chutney

2 cups mint leaves, chopped
1 cup chopped coriander
½ cup onions, sliced
juice of 1 to 2 lemons
1 tablespoon sugar
4 to 6 green chillies
salt to taste

Preparation time :
10 minutes.

No Cooking.

Makes 1 cup.

1. Combine all the ingredients and grind to a smooth paste in a blender using very little water.
2. Refrigerate and use as required.

Handy tip : *You can even make a tangy dip out of this chutney by adding 1 cup of whisked curds to half a cup of this chutney. Serve it with papads or wafers to make a quick appetizer.*

Guacamole

1 cup ripe avocado pulp
juice of ½ lemon
¼ cup onions, finely chopped
¼ cup tomatoes, finely chopped
1 green chilli, finely chopped
1 tablespoon chopped coriander
salt to taste

**Preparation time :
10 minutes.**

No Cooking.

Makes 1½ cups.

1. Combine all the ingredients in a bowl and mash well using a fork.
2. Refrigerate till required.
   Serve chilled.

Handy tip : *If the avocados are not ripe, store them in a jar of rice or a brown paper bag to ripen completely before using them to make guacamole.*

Khajur Imli Ki Chutney

2 cups dates (khajur), deseeded
¼ cup tamarind (imli), deseeded
1 cup jaggery (gur), grated
1 teaspoon chilli powder
½ teaspoon black salt (sanchal)
a pinch asafoetida (hing)
salt to taste

Preparation time :
10 minutes.

Cooking time :
25 minutes.

Makes 2 cups.

1. Wash the dates and tamarind and place them in a saucepan.
2. Add the jaggery, chilli powder, black salt, asafoetida, salt and 4 cups of water and simmer for 20 to 25 minutes.
3. Cool and blend the mixture in a liquidiser adding a little water if required to make a smooth paste.
4. Strain through a sieve and use as required. Store refrigerated.

Grilled Eggplant Dip

Preparation time :
5 minutes.

Cooking time :
15 minutes.

Makes 1½ cups.

1 large (½ kg.) eggplant (brinjal)
¾ cup tomatoes, finely chopped
3 tablespoons finely chopped parsley
1 teaspoon garlic, finely grated
1 teaspoon lemon juice
¼ cup onions, finely chopped
1 teaspoon cumin (jeera) powder
salt to taste
oil for greasing

For serving
pita bread or cream crackers

1. Pierce the eggplant with a knife or fork and grease lightly with some oil.
2. Grill over a charcoal or electric barbeque till the insides are soft and pulpy.
3. Peel the skin off and discard.
4. Place the pulp in a bowl and mash well using a fork.
5. Add the tomatoes, parsley, garlic, lemon juice, onions, cumin powder and salt and mix well.
6. Refrigerate for at least 1 hour before serving. Serve with pita bread or cream crackers.

Barbeque Sauce

Preparation time :
5 minutes.

Cooking time :
20 minutes.

Makes ¾ cup.

2 teaspoons vinegar
1 teaspoon lemon juice
½ cup water
½ cup onions, finely chopped
2 tablespoons sugar
¼ cup butter
½ teaspoon freshly crushed pepper
½ cup tomato ketchup
1 teaspoon salt
2 tablespoons Worcestershire sauce
¼ teaspoon chilli flakes

For the smoking
1 piece charcoal
1 teaspoon butter

1. Combine all the ingredients in a saucepan and bring to a boil. Allow to simmer for about 10 to 12 minutes.
2. Heat the charcoal over a gas till it is red hot and place it in a small bowl.
3. Place this bowl in the saucepan that contains the sauce, pour the butter over the coal and cover it immediately. Leave aside for 5 to 10 minutes.
4. Remove the bowl containing the coal and discard. Serve warm.

Spring Onion & Curd Dip

1 cup fresh thick curds
4 spring onions, chopped
1 teaspoon garlic, chopped
½ teaspoon cumin seeds (jeera) powder
1 green chilli, chopped
salt to taste

Preparation time :
5 minutes.

No Cooking.

Makes 1½ cups.

1. Combine all the ingredients in a blender and blend till it is smooth.
2. Refrigerate till required.
   Serve chilled with vegetable crudites or any barbequed dish of your choice.